Thomas Hardy, son of a rustic Dorset builder, was to become an architect, poet, novelist, playwright and essayist. In short, he was a genius, a fact made all the more surprising by his unpromising start in life.

NOTE: *Prose extracts in Hardy's own words appear in italic type.*

Born 2 June 1840, at Higher Bockhampton, near Dorchester, *the smallest and feeblest of folk there,* he was a sickly child, not expected to live past his first years. His childhood, however, was dominated by the rural, domestic events that he would later recall in his poetry, novels and short stories and by the tale-telling and gossip of his elders, and by games and rambles. All of these provided the conditions that Hardy saw as necessary to give meaning to life in an isolated place. He describes them in detail in *The Woodlanders.*

*They are old associations – an almost exhaustive biographical or historical acquaintance with every object, animate or inanimate, within the observer's horizon. He must know all about those invisible ones of the days gone by, whose feet have traversed the fields which look so grey from his windows; recall whose creaking plough has turned those sods from time to time; whose hands planted the trees that form a crest to the opposite hill; whose horses and hounds have torn through that underwood; what birds affect that particular brake; what bygone domestic dramas of love, jealousy, revenge, or disappointment have been enacted in the cottages, the mansion, the street or on the green.*

In this short book we try to give some insight into the importance of Wessex to Thomas Hardy, particularly in his most well-known novels.

## 'REE

# Life in an Isolated Place

The Hardy family home had been built by Thomas's great-grandfather, Thomas the First, for his son, Thomas the Second. 'Standing alone, mud walls and thatched' as an insurance policy of 1829 described it, the cottage was unusual for the time because it was inhabited by a single family – Thomas Hardy (the Second), his wife Jemima, and their four children of whom the oldest, Thomas, was to immortalise it.

It stood in a spot remote enough for it to be used as a smuggler's store for brandy landed between Weymouth and Lulworth Cove. Egdon Heath lay to the east, a vast and wild territory, which played a prominent part in *The Return of the Native* in particular.

The garden was large enough for the cultivation of vegetables, apples (gathered for the cider-maker with his *mill, and tubs, and vat, and press*), a pig for killing and salting each autumn, beehives for honey and sometimes, for carrying heavy goods, a horse.

### The Ghost of the Past

We two kept house, the Past and I,
      The Past and I;
Through all my tasks it hovered nigh,
      Leaving me never alone.
It was a spectral housekeeping
      Where fell no jarring tone,
As strange, as still a housekeeping
      As ever has been known.

As daily I went up the stair
      And down the stair,
I did not mind the Bygone there –
      The Present once to me;
Its moving meek companionship
      I wished might ever be,
There was in that companionship
      Something of ecstasy.

It dwelt with me just as it was,
      Just as it was
When first its prospects gave me pause
      In wayward wanderings,
Before the years had torn old troths
      As they tear all sweet things,
Before gaunt griefs had torn old troths
      And dulled old rapturings.

And then its form began to fade,
      Began to fade,
Its gentle echoes faintlier played
      At eves upon my ear
Than when the autumn's look embrowned
      The lonely chambers here,
When autumn's setting shades embrowned
      Nooks that it haunted near.

And so with time my vision less,
      Yea, less and less
Makes of that Past my housemistress,
      It dwindles in my eye;
It looms a far-off skeleton
      And not a comrade nigh,
A fitful far-off skeleton
      Dimming as days draw by.

Below:
*The choirmaster here referred to was Thomas Hardy I, the poet's grandfather. He was the founder of the village choir at Stinsford church; the sketch shows the interior at that time. Thomas Hardy II, the poet's father, was the 'tenor man'.*

### The Choirmaster's Burial

He often would ask us
That, when he died,
After playing so many
To their last rest,
If out of us any
Should here abide,
And it would not task us,
We would with our lutes
Play over him
By his grave-brim
The psalm he liked best –
The one whose sense suits
'Mount Ephraim' –
And perhaps we should seem
To him, in Death's dream,
Like the seraphim.

As soon as I knew
That his spirit was gone
I thought this his due,
And spoke thereupon.
'I think,' said the vicar,
'A read service quicker
Than viols out-of-doors
In these frosts and hoars.
That old-fashioned way
Requires a fine day,
And it seems to me
It had better not be.'

Hence, that afternoon,
Though never knew he
That his wish could not be,
To get through it faster
They buried the master
Without any tune.

But 'twas said that, when
At the dead of next night
The vicar looked out,
There struck on his ken
Thronged roundabout,
Where the frost was graying
The headstoned grass,
A band all in white
Like the saints in church-glass,
Singing and playing
The ancient stave
By the choirmaster's grave.

Such the tenor man told
When he had grown old.

Music was important – both his father and grandfather were members of the Stinsford church choir, near Bockhampton. Hardy the writer also sang in the choir, which in those days was accompanied by viola and not the 'new-fangled' organ of later days. He was to recall these musical experiences through the members of the Mellstock quire in *Under the Greenwood Tree*.

During Hardy's childhood the labourer was always on the edge of pauperism and women like Tess (of the d'Urbervilles) would often have to be employed, as she was, on threshing machines and at such heavy tasks as swede-hacking.

*The swede-field in which she and her companion were set hacking was a stretch of a hundred odd acres, in one patch, on the highest ground of the farm, rising above stony lanchets or lynchets – the outcrop of siliceous veins in the chalk formation, composed of myriads of loose white flints in bulbous, cusped, and phallic shapes. The upper half of each turnip had been eaten off by the live-stock, and it was the business of the two women to grub up the lower or earthy half of the root with a hooked fork called a hacker, that it might be eaten also. …In the afternoon the rain came on again.*

*…There are degrees of dampness, and a very little is called being wet through in common talk. But to stand working slowly in a field, and feel the creep of rain-water, first in legs and shoulders, then on hips and head, then at back, front, and sides, and yet to work on till the leaden light diminishes and marks that the sun is down, demands a distinct modicum of stoicism, even of valour.*

The Reverend Charles Kegan Paul wrote, as late as 1868, that 'Wages are so low that a man with children above eight years old is glad of the few shillings which may be earned by them, and the employers of labour insist on these boys being sent into the fields, even if the parents would willingly make an effort to keep them at school. The farmer finds it pays him well to get two boys who, under a man, will do a man's work, but whose combined work costs less than an able-bodied man's wages.'

*Left:*
*Thomas Hardy (the writer) played the violin and accordion. 'The Dorchester Hornpipe' was found in a music book of his.*

*Below:*
*In this poem, written in 1915, the 'lonely barton by yonder coomb' was built by Hardy's father.*

### The Oxen

Christmas Eve, and twelve of the clock.
　'Now they are all on their knees,'
An elder said as we sat in a flock
　By the embers in hearthside ease.

We pictured the meek mild creatures where
　They dwelt in their strawy pen,
Nor did it occur to one of us there
　To doubt they were kneeling then.

So fair a fancy few would weave
　In these years! Yet, I feel,
If someone said on Christmas Eve,
　'Come; see the oxen kneel

'In the lonely barton by yonder coomb
　Our childhood used to know,'
I should go with him in the gloom,
　Hoping it might be so.

# Marriage HARDY–GIFFORD *Sept. 17, St. Peter's Church*

*Lulworth Cove, the scene on the Dorset coast of Frank Troy's supposed disappearance.*

Hardy's architectural career lasted from the time he left school (1856) until (1872). This quiet, small, but no longer delicate, young man, fell in love with Emma Lavinia Gifford. Their wedding took place in London, on 17 September, at St. Peter's Church, Paddington, largely because of the hostility between the respective families. The only existing reference by Hardy to the ceremony is in the marriages column of the Dorset County Chronicle, 24 September 1874, as given above. The tension between Hardy's mother, who exerted a strong influence over him, and Emma, whom he had met when he was a young architect in St. Juliot, Cornwall, never abated and, in many ways, Jemima Hardy provided food for her son's writing.

*Far from the Madding Crowd* was Hardy's first published novel after his marriage.

... '*I am perfectly convinced that he is still alive.*'

*Bathsheba remained firm in this opinion till Monday, when two circumstances conjoined to shake it. The first was a short paragraph in the local newspaper, which, beyond making by a methodizing pen formidable presumptive evidence of Troy's death by drowning, contained the important testimony of a young Mr. Barker, M.D., of Budmouth, who spoke of being an eyewitness of the accident, in a letter to the editor. In this he stated that he was passing over the cliff on the remoter side of the cove just as the sun was setting. At that time he saw a bather carried along in the current outside the mouth of the cove, and guessed in an instant that there was but a poor chance for him unless he should be possessed of unusual muscular*

*powers. He drifted behind a projection of the coast, and Mr. Barker followed along the shore in the same direction. But by the time that he could reach an elevation sufficiently great to command a view of the sea beyond, dusk had set in, and nothing further was to be seen.*

*The other circumstance was the arrival of his clothes…*

*Below:*

*The King's Arms Hotel, Dorchester, was the old coaching inn into which Boldwood carried Bathsheba, who had fainted on being told of the death of her husband.*

He entered the gravel path which would take him behind the tower. The path, instead of being stony as it had been the night before, was browned over with a thin coating of mud. At one place in the path he saw a tuft of stringy roots washed white and clean as a bundle of tendons. He picked it up — surely it could not be one of the primroses he had planted? He saw a bulb, another, and another as he advanced. Beyond doubt they were the crocuses. With a face of perplexed dismay Troy turned the corner and then beheld the wreck the stream had made.

The pool upon the grave had soaked away into the ground, and in its place was a hollow. The disturbed earth was washed over the grass and

PUDDLETOWN.

*pathway in the guise of the brown mud he had already seen, and it spotted the marble tombstone with the same stains. Nearly all the flowers were washed clean out of the ground, and they lay, roots upwards, on the spots whither they had been splashed by the stream….*

*He slowly withdrew from the grave. He did not attempt to fill up the hole, replace the flowers, or do anything at all. He simply threw up his cards and forswore his game for that time and always. Going out of the churchyard silently and unobserved – none of the villagers having yet risen – he passed down some fields at the back, and emerged just as secretly upon the high road. Shortly afterwards he had gone from the village.*

**Below:**

*It was in the churchyard of Puddletown Church that Frank Troy planted flowers on the grave of Fanny Robin, only to find that the rain would cruelly wash them away. After this, he had no desire to return to his old life with Bathsheba.*

# THE RETURN OF THE NATIVE

*Egdon Heath covered a vast tract of Dorset. Six years before Hardy's birth, the Tolpuddle martyrs had been sentenced to transportation for attempting to organise a primitive agricultural trade union just a few miles across the heath from Bockhampton. Dorset was described in a guidebook of*

Thomas Hardy lived in many places between his childhood in Higher Bockhampton (1840–56), irregular and sometimes lengthy visits there (1856–74), and his last home, Max Gate (1885–1928), which he designed and had built for him. He and Emma spent two happy years in Riverside Villa, Sturminster Newton, during the early part of their marriage. At this time, Hardy wrote *The Return of the Native.*

*He walked along towards home without attending to paths. If any one knew the heath well it was Clym. He was permeated with its scenes, with its substance, and with its odours. He might be said to be its product. His eyes had first opened thereon; with its appearance all the first images of his*

*memory were mingled; his estimate of life had been coloured by it; his toys had been the flint knives and arrow-heads which he found there, wondering why stones should 'grow' to such odd shapes; his flowers, the purple bells and yellow furze; his animal kingdom, the snakes and croppers; his society, its human haunters. Take all the varying hates felt by Eustacia Vye towards the heath, and translate them into loves, and you have the heart of Clym. He gazed upon the wide prospect as he walked, and was glad.*

*To many persons this Egdon was a place which had slipped out of its century generations ago, to intrude as an uncouth object into this. It was an obsolete thing and few cared to study it.*

*1856 as 'a bleak county of chalk downs and sandy heaths, thinly peopled, and below the average of the English counties in fertility', although it had 'a certain charm in its very wildness and the forlorn aspect of its villages'. Hardy's description of it seems to bear this out.*

*Below:*

*Hardy was a frequent visitor to the new Dorset Museum in Dorchester (the building just beyond the awning) after his move back to the town in 1883. He spent many hours in the library, writing the* Mayor of Casterbridge. *(Casterbridge was Hardy's name for Dorchester.)*

The years 1878–83 were passed in Tooting, London, and Wimborne, interspersed with holidays in Dorset, Normandy and Cambridge. Thomas and Emma did not find life anywhere so satisfactory as in Dorset, so in June 1883 they returned to Dorchester.

On the first day of 1884 the Dorset County Museum opened the doors to the premises it occupies still. Hardy immediately became a frequent visitor to the handsome reading room with its daily supply of London newspapers and numerous works on historical, philosophical and literary topics. He was already a member of the Dorset Natural History and Antiquarian Field Club (the great Iron Age hill fort, Maiden Castle, and other archaeological sites feature in his works), and by June 1884 had been appointed a local magistrate. Also at this time Hardy began to write *The Mayor of Casterbridge.*

*Right:*

*William Barnes, the Dorset poet, lived in Came rectory (still visible but not visitable). Hardy described him as 'probably the most interesting link between present and past forms of rural life that England possessed'. He was 'a complete repertory of forgotten manners, words, and sentiments'.*

*A few score yards brough them to the spot where th town band was now shaking the window panes with the strains ( 'The Roast Beef of Ol England.'*

*The building befor whose doors they ha pitched their music stands was the chief hote in Casterbridge – namely the King's Arms. A spa cious bow-window pro jected into the street ove the main portico, an from the open sashe came the babble of voices the jingle of glasses, an the drawing of corks.*

*. . .'That's M r Henchard, the Mayor, ( the end of the table, ( facing ye;'*

# HARDY'S WESSEX PLACE-NAMES

| HARDY'S NAME | REAL NAME | HARDY'S NAME | REAL NAME |
|---|---|---|---|
| Abbott's Cernel | Cerne Abbas | Longpuddle | Piddletrenthide |
| Abbotsea | Abbotsbury | Lornton | Hornton |
| Aldbrickham | Reading | Lulwind Cove | Lulworth Cove |
| Alderworth | Briantspuddle | Lumsdon | Cumnor |
| Alfredston | Wantage | | |
| Anglebury | Wareham | Markton | Dunster |
| Arrowthorne | Minstead | Marlbury | Marlborough |
| Athelhall | Athelhampton | Marlott | Marnhull |
| | | Marshwood | Middlemarsh |
| Broad Sidlinch | Sidling St. Nicholas | Marygreen | Fawley |
| Budmouth Regis | Weymouth | Melchester | Salisbury |
| Bulbarrow | A hill near Sturminster Newton | Mellstock | Stinsford/Bockhampton |
| | | Melport | Weymouth |
| | | Middleton Abbey | Milton Abbas |
| Camelton | Camelford | Montislope | Montacute |
| Carriford | Stinsford/Bockhampton | Moreford | Moreton |
| Casterbridge | Dorchester | | |
| Castle Boterel | Boscastle | Narroborne | West Coker |
| Chalk-Newton | Maiden Newton | Nether Moynton | Owermoigne |
| Charmley | Charminster | Newland Buckton | Buckland Newton |
| Chaseborough | Cranborne | Norcombe Hill | A hill near Toller Down |
| Chene Manor | Canford Magna | Nuttlebury | Hazelbury Bryan |
| Christminster | Oxford | | |
| Cliff Martin | Coombe Martin | Oakbury Fitzpiers | Okeford Fitzpaine |
| Clyfton Horseleigh | Clifton Maybank | Oozewood | Ringwood |
| Corvsgate | Corfe Castle | Overcombe | Sutton Poyntz |
| Cresscombe | Letcombe Basset | Owlscombe | Batcombe |
| Creston | Preston | Oxwell | Poxwell |
| | | | |
| Damer's Wood | Came Wood near Dorchester | Pen-zephyr | Penzance |
| | | Port Bredy | Bridport |
| Delborough | East Chelborough | Po'sham | Portesham |
| Dogbury | A hill near High Stoy | | |
| Downstaple | Barnstaple | Redrutin | Redruth |
| Durnover | Fordington | Ringsworth | Ringstead |
| | | Rookington | Hurn |
| East Egdon | Affpuddle | Roy-Town | Troytown |
| East Endelstow | Lesnewth | | |
| Egdon Heath | A composite of the heaths between Bournemouth and Dorchester | St. Launces | Launceston |
| | | St. Maria's | St. Mary's, Isles of Scilly |
| | | Sandbourne | Bournemouth |
| | | Scrimpton | Frampton |
| Elm Cranlynch | Corfe Mullen | Shadwater | Woodsford |
| Emminster | Beaminster | Shaston | Shaftesbury |
| Evershead | Evershot | Sherton Abbas | Sherborne |
| Exonbury | Exeter | Shottsford Forum | Blandford Forum |
| | | Silverthorne | Up Exe |
| Fensworth | Letcombe Regis | Sleeping Green | Carhampton or Withycombe |
| Flintcomb-Ash | Plush | | |
| Flychett | Lytchett Minster | Solentsea | Southsea |
| Fountall | Wells | Springham | Warmwell |
| Froom-Everard | West Stafford | Stagfoot Lane | Hartfoot Lane: Melcombe Bingham |
| Gaymead | Shinfield | | |
| Giant's Town | Hugh Town, Isles of Scilly | Stapleford | Stalbridge |
| Great Hintock | Melbury Bubb/Minterne Magna | Stickleford | Tincleton |
| | | Stoke Barehills | Basingstoke |
| | | Stourcastle | Sturminster Newton |
| Havenpool | Poole | Street of Wells | Fortuneswell |
| Holmstoke | East Stoke/East Holme /West Holme | Tivworthy | Tiverton |
| | | Tolchurch | Tolpuddle |
| Idmouth | Sidmouth | Tollamore | Stinsford/Bockhampton |
| Isle of Slingers | Portland | Toneborough | Taunton |
| Isles of Lyonesse | Isles of Scilly | Tor-upon-Sea | Torquay |
| Ivell | Yeovil | Trantridge | Pentridge |
| | | Trufal | Truro |
| Kennetbridge | Newbury | | |
| Kingsbere-sub-Greenhill | Bere Regis | Warborne | Wimborne Minster |
| Kingscreech | Creech | Weatherbury | Puddletown |
| King's Hintock | Melbury Osmund | Welland | Charborough |
| Knapwater | Kingsbury Maurward | Wellbridge | Woolbridge |
| Knollingwood | Wimborne St. Giles | West Endelstow | St. Juliot |
| Knollsea | Swanage | Weydon Priors | Weyhill |
| | | Wherryborne | Winterborne Came |
| Leddenton | Gillingham | Wintoncester | Winchester |
| Lew Everard | West Stafford | Wyndway | Upton |
| Little Enckworth | Kingston | | |
| Little Hintock | Stockwood/Hermitage | Yalbury Wood | Yellowham Wood |

Cliff without name
Targan Bay
Dundagel
Nallency Vale
St. Launce's
Plymouth

*Fictitious names as*
*Exonbury*
*Real names as*
*Portsmouth*

0   5   10   15 Miles

OFF WESSEX

Trufal

Penzephyr

Lands End

Channel

Stancy Castle

Bristol

Mendip
Hills

Bat

B r i s t o l

Exon Moor
Dunkery
Beacon

Quantock
Hills

Sedgemoor

Fountall

Glaston

O U E R

W E S S E X

Downstaple

L O W E R

Tonshorough

Ivell

Shert
Abba

Vale of B

Tivworthy

King's
Kintock
Emminster
Pilsdon
Chalk
Newton

Hig
Sto

River Axe

Exonbury

W E S S E X

Idmouth

Port Bredy

S O U T H

Casterbridge

Blackon

Jae

Deadmans Bay

Tor-upon-Sea

T h e

Isle of Slingers

The Beal

Th
Ra

☐ CORNWALL   ☐ BERKSHIRE   ☐ DEVON   ☐ DORSET   ☐ GLOUCEST

ThomasHardy's WESSEX

Christminster
Lumsdon

NORTH

Alfredston

Marygreen

WESSEX

MID

Marlbury Downs

Castle Royal
Aldbrickham

Batton Castle

Kennetbridge

Inkpen Beacon

Stoke Barehills

Quartershot

WESSEX

Weydon Priors

Icenway House

The Great

Stonehenge

UPPER

Plain

ourMead

Melchester

Wintoncester

Wingreen

Trantridge Cross

Deansleigh

The Chase

WESSEX

rcastle

Chaseborough

Southampton

oreShottsford

Forum

Lornton Inn

barrow

Worborne

The Great

omb-Ash

Chene Manor

Heath

Havenpool

Forest

Solentsea

From

Sandbourne

The Island

Portsmouth

Anglebury

Wellbridge

Knollsea

ship

Channel

5   0   5   10   15 Miles

RE    HAMPSHIRE    OXFORDSHIRE    SOMERSET    WILTSHIRE

Septentrio
Oriens
Occidens
Meridies

Soon after finishing *The Mayor of Casterbridge*, Hardy was at work on another novel, *The Woodlanders*, which he finished early in 1887.

Hardy made his most important house removal – to Max Gate, Wareham Road, Dorchester – on 29 June 1885 and, five months later, began writing *The Woodlanders*. After it was published in 1887 it attracted enthusiastic reviews. Hardy himself preferred its story to any other of his novels. Perhaps this was because it drew heavily on memories of his mother's talk and the qualities he had admired in his father, which found expression in the character of Giles Winterborne.

**Right:**

*Two word-pictures from* The Woodlanders *describing different aspects of rural life.*

**Below:**

*The village of Okeford Fitzpaine around the turn of the century. This is one of the three Okeford villages immortalized by the village of* Oakbury-Fitzpiers, *in* The Woodlanders.

*Winterborne was standing in front of the brick oven in his shirt-sleeves, tossing in thorn-sprays, and stirring about the blazing mass with a long-handled, three-pronged Beelzebub kind of fork, the heat shining out upon his streaming face and making his eyes like furnaces; the thorns crackling and sputtering; while Creedle, having ranged the pastry dishes in a row on the table till the oven should be ready, was pressing out the crust of a final apple-pie with a rolling-pin. A great pot boiled on the fire; and through the open door of the back-kitchen a boy was seen seated on the fender, emptying the snuffers and scouring the candlesticks, a row of the latter standing upside down on the hob to melt out the grease.*

*The horses wore their bells that day. There were sixteen to the team, carried on a frame above each animal's shoulders, and tuned to scale, so as to form two octaves, running from the highest note on the right or off-side of the leader to the lowest on the left or near-side of the shaft-horse. Melbury was among the last to retain horse-bells in that neighbourhood; for living at Little Hintock, where the lanes yet remained as narrow as before the days of turnpike roads, these sound-signals were still as useful to him and his neighbours as they had ever been in former times. Much backing was saved in the course of a year by the warning notes they cast ahead; moreover, the tones of all the teams in the district being known to the carters of each, they could tell a long way off on a dark night whether they were about to encounter friends or strangers.*

# TESS OF THE D'URBERVILLES

*A fine 16th-century bridge over the Frome adjoins Woolbridge Manor House, which once belonged to a branch of the Turberville family. After their marriage Tess and Angel stay at* Wellbridge *in an old farmhouse by a great Elizabethan bridge.*

Hardy's next full-length novel was *Tess of the d'Urbervilles*. The character of Tess was largely formed through memories of past (including childhood) experiences. Many of the events, too, were drawn from childhood associations, but as was his normal custom when working on a novel, the landscape within which the book was set was not re-visited by Hardy during his writing.

## Tess's Lament

I

I would that folk forgot me quite,
 Forgot me quite!
I would that I could shrink from sight,
 And no more see the sun.
Would it were time to say farewell,
To claim my nook, to need my knell,
Time for them all to stand and tell
 Of my day's work as done.

II

Ah! dairy where I lived so long,
 I lived so long;
Where I would rise up staunch and strong,
 And lie down hopefully.
'Twas there within the chimney-seat
He watched me to the clock's slow beat –
Loved me, and learnt to call me Sweet,
 And whispered words to me.

III

And now he's gone; and now he's gone;...
 And now he's gone!
The flowers we potted perhaps are thrown
 To rot upon the farm.
And where we had our supper-fire
May now grow nettle, dock, and briar,
And all the place be mould and mire
 So cozy once and warm.

IV

And it was I who did it all,
 Who did it all;
'Twas I who made the blow to fall
 On him who thought no guile.
Well, it is finished – past, and he
Has left me to my misery,
And I must take my Cross on me
 For wronging him awhile.

V

How gay we looked that day we wed,
 That day we wed!
'May joy be with ye!' they all said
 A-standing by the durn.
I wonder what they say o' us now,
And if they know my lot; and how
She feels who milks my favourite cow,
 And takes my place at churn!

VI

It wears me out to think of it,
 To think of it;
I cannot bear my fate as writ,
 I'd have my life unbe;
Would turn my memory to a blot,
Make every relic of me rot,
My doings be as they were not,
 And gone all trace of me!

The last of Hardy's novels, and his most socially conscious, *Jude the Obscure*, was written in 1893–94. Although *The Well-Beloved* did not appear until 1897, it had been written ten years earlier.

*Jude the Obscure* was first published in serial form and the publishers, because they could print 'nothing which could not be read aloud in any family circle', were constrained to alter it quite drastically. Later, when published in its complete form in November 1985, Hardy was 'unprepared for the depth, extent, and directness of the hostility which marked many of the reviews'. The *Guardian* described it as 'a shameful nightmare which one only wishes to forget as quickly and as completely as possible'. The critic, Edmund Gosse, wrote 'It is a very gloomy, it is even a grimy, story that Mr. Hardy has at last presented to his admirers...' Hardy replied, *The 'grimy' features of the story go to show the contrast between the ideal life a man wished to lead, and the squalid real life he was fated to lead... It is, in fact, to be discovered in every body's life...*

*Below left:*
*Shaftesbury*, Shaston, *features in* Tess of the d'Urbervilles, *because Tess goes there to board a carrier's cart to Trantridge so that she can work for the Stoke d'Urbervilles, and in* Jude the Obscure, *Jude enters on the summit of the peak after a toilsome climb; Sue and Richard Phillston's school building in Bimport Street were extensive and stone-built; whilst waiting for lessons to finish, Jude withdrew a few steps along Abbey Walk...[then] walked down to the level terrace where the Abbey gardens once had spread and later on missed his coach which had left from* The Duke's Arms, *The Grosvenor Hotel. Whilst waiting for another, he walked through the venerable graveyard of Trinity Church, with its avenues of limes (now the Trinity Centre).*

# JUDE THE OBSCURE

*Christminster*, Oxford.

*He now paused at the top of a crooked and gentle declivity, and obtained his first near view of the city. Grey stoned and dun-roofed, it stood within hail of the Wessex border, and almost with the tip of one small toe within it, at the northern-most point of the crinkled line along which the leisurely*

*Thames strokes the fields of that ancient kingdom. The buildings now lay quiet in the sunset, a vane here and there on their many spires and domes giving sparkle to a picture of sober secondary and tertiary hues.*

### A Cathedral Façade at Midnight

Along the sculptures of the western wall
  I watched the moonlight creeping:
It moved as if it hardly moved at all,
  Inch by inch thinly peeping
Round on the pious figures of freestone, brought
And poised there when the Universe was wrought
To serve its centre, Earth, in mankind's thought.

The lunar look skimmed scantly toe, breast, arm,
  Then edged on slowly, slightly,
To shoulder, hand, face; till each austere form
  Was blanched its whole length brightly
Of prophet, king, queen, cardinal in state,
That dead men's tools had striven to simulate;
And the stiff images stood irradiate.

A frail moan from the martyred saints there set
  Mid others of the erection
Against the breeze, seemed sighings of regret
  At the ancient faith's rejection
Under the sure, unhasting, steady stress
Of Reason's movement, making meaningless
The coded creeds of old-time godliness.

*Right:*
*Hardy visited Salisbury
in 1860, probably to
accompany his sister
Mary on her admission to
Salisbury Training
College (in the King's
House in the Close,
which now houses the
Salisbury and South
Wiltshire Museum) and
on a holiday in 1897.
The pleasure he felt in the
peacefulness of the Close
is reflected in the poem
printed here.*
 *Jude, like Hardy, was
a stonemason and he
moved to Melchester,*
Salisbury, *hoping to get
work on the restoration of
the cathedral. Christopher
Julian in* The Hand
of Ethelberta,

*published in 1876, is the cathedral organist, and the city is mentioned in several other of Hardy's stories, notably 'On the Western Circuit' (1891) and 'A Committee Man of "The Terror"'(1896).*

**Left:**
*The King's House was a familiar place to Hardy's family.*

Hardy wrote very little more until after the sudden and unexpected death of Emma, his first wife, in 1912. Many of his poems refer nostalgically to the time of their courtship; they were written in his later years.

His second wife, Florence, whom he married in 1914, looked after him until his death on 11 January 1928. His ashes are laid in Poets' Corner, Westminster Abbey, but his heart is buried in Emma's grave at Stinsford, next to the tombs of his parents.

# Postscript

The story of Tess, even more than that of Jude, seems to show with haunting certainty 'the sheer irrevocability of moments of decision and choice – the opportunity lost, the word unuttered, the road not taken, the beloved recognized or reclaimed too late. It is upon such moments, explored in all their irony and despair, that so many of [Hardy's] novels and stories turn, and some of the most poignant of his personal poems. Almost always it is a woman who pays' (Millgate, 1989).

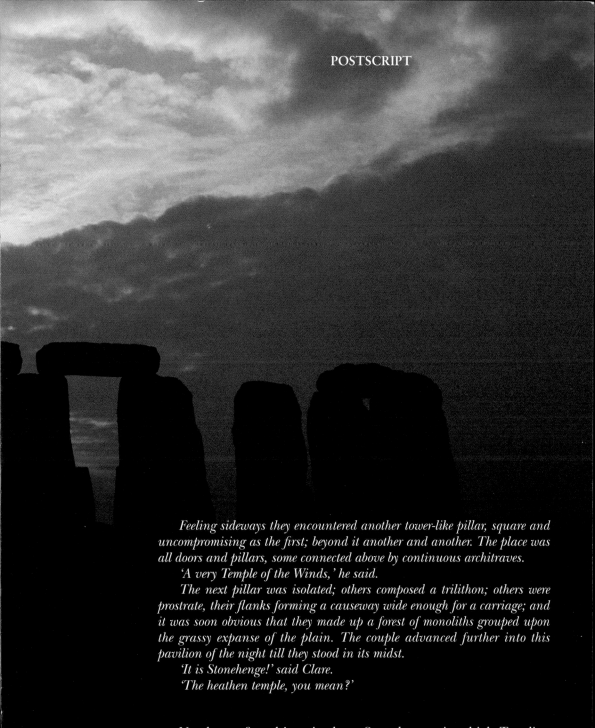

*Feeling sideways they encountered another tower-like pillar, square and uncompromising as the first; beyond it another and another. The place was all doors and pillars, some connected above by continuous architraves.*

*'A very Temple of the Winds,' he said.*

*The next pillar was isolated; others composed a trilithon; others were prostrate, their flanks forming a causeway wide enough for a carriage; and it was soon obvious that they made up a forest of monoliths grouped upon the grassy expanse of the plain. The couple advanced further into this pavilion of the night till they stood in its midst.*

*'It is Stonehenge!' said Clare.*

*'The heathen temple, you mean?'*

Not long after this episode at Stonehenge, in which Tess lies exhausted on the altar stone, she is arrested and pays the ultimate price in Winchester gaol. *A few minutes after the hour had struck something moved slowly up the staff, and extended itself upon the breeze. It was a black flag.*

After the Last Breath

There's no more to be done, or feared, or hoped;
None now need watch, speak low, and list, and tire;
No irksome crease outsmoothed, no pillow sloped
    Does she require.

Blankly we gaze. We are free to go or stay;
Our morrow's anxious plans have missed their aim;
Whether we leave to-night or wait till day
    Counts as the same.

The lettered vessels of medicaments
Seem asking wherefore we have set them here;
Each palliative its silly face presents
    As useless gear.

And yet we feel that something savours well;
We note a numb relief withheld before;
Our well-beloved is prisoner in the cell
    Of Time no more.

We see by littles now the deft achievement
Whereby she has escaped the Wrongers all,
In view of which our momentary bereavement
    Outshapes but small.

Desmond Hawkins, *Thomas Hardy, His life and Landscape*, The National Trust, 1990

Denys Kay-Robinson, *The Landscape of Thomas Hardy*, Webb & Bower, 1984

Michael Millgate, *Thomas Hardy, A biography*, O.U.P., 1982

F.P.Pitfield, *Hardy's Wessex Locations*, Dorset Publishing Company, 1992

David Wright (ed.), *Thomas Hardy, Selected Poems*, Penguin Books, 1978

*Left:*
*Hardy's mother lived until after he had written his last novel and almost all his stories. She was always a very significant influence on all his published works.*

## WESSEX BOOKS

Watch out for other titles in
THE WESSEX SERIES

- Vineyards of Wessex
- Crop Circles of Wessex
- Prehistoric Sacred Sites of Wessex, Vol. I
- King Arthur in Wessex
- Women of Wessex • Haunted Wessex
- The Story of Wessex
- Jane Austen in Wessex
- Great Religious Houses of Wessex
- Travellers in Wessex
from:
Wessex Books, 2 Station Cottages,
Newton Toney, Salisbury,
Wiltshire SP4 0HD
Telephone 01980 629349
Facsimile 01980 629599

### Acknowledgements

For the use of illustrations and photographs the publishers gratefully thank:

Dorset Natural History and Archaeological Society, pp. 4, 28, back cover.
Terry Linee, front cover, p.2;
Simon McBride, pp. 6, 10, 18, 22;
Kim Williams Photography, p.26.

Line drawings by John Fuller.
Cover illustration by Andrew Stewart Jamieson.
Cover panel and centre map, design and computer typesetting produced by Alexander S. Grenfell.
(Map based on Thomas Hardy's Wessex in Pocket Papermac, published by Macmillan & Co. Ltd.)
Written by Jane Drake.

Published by Wessex Books 1997.
Text © Jane Drake.

Printed in Great Britain by B.A.S. Printers.

ISBN 0 9529619 2 X

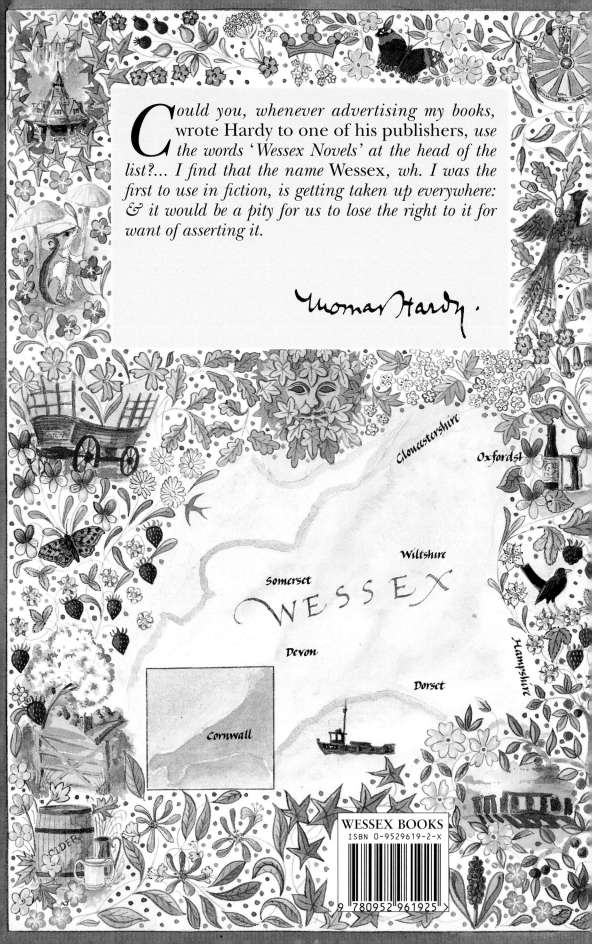

*C*ould you, whenever advertising my books, wrote Hardy to one of his publishers, *use the words 'Wessex Novels' at the head of the list?... I find that the name* Wessex, *wh. I was the first to use in fiction, is getting taken up everywhere: & it would be a pity for us to lose the right to it for want of asserting it.*

Thomas Hardy.

Gloucestershire

Oxfordsh

Wiltshire

Somerset

WESSEX

Devon

Hampshire

Dorset

Cornwall

WESSEX BOOKS
ISBN 0-9529619-2-X

9 780952 961925